TAKE A HIKE!

AROUND AN AMAZING WORLD

RICHARD MERRITT

www.littleharebooks.com

For Mum, Dad and Louise—RM

Little Hare Books
8/21 Mary Street, Surry Hills
NSW 2010 AUSTRALIA

www.littleharebooks.com

First published in 2008

National Library of Australia
Cataloguing-in-Publication entry
Merritt, Richard, 1982-.
Take a hike!: around an amazing world.

For primary school children.
ISBN 978 1 921049 85 9 (pbk.).

1. Travel - Juvenile literature. 2. Maze puzzles - Juvenile literature. I. Title.

910

Designed by Bernadette Gethings
Produced in Singapore by Pica Digital
Printed in China through Phoenix Offset

5 4 3 2 1

TAKE A HIKE!

Are you ready for the trip of a lifetime?

It's time to begin an amazing journey around the world! You'll witness the most spectacular sights you'll ever see. Be prepared to climb up mountains, travel across icebergs and explore cities. Get ready to encounter the greatest places that the world has to offer!

It won't be easy finding your way through—it's a maze out there! Look out for the green arrow and red cross on every puzzle. They show you the beginning and end point of each trek. It's up to you to find a clear route. If something gets in the way, like a fallen tree or a lazy tiger, then you'll have to find another path.

Keep your eyes peeled to count the special objects in each area. They could be animals, food, or even kites—but you won't know until you get there! And there's something not quite right about the places you'll visit... They each have an object, animal or building that doesn't belong. Can you spot it?

If you fall in love with the places you're visiting, you can check out more amazing facts at the back of the book, just before the solutions.

So come on then, what are you waiting for!

LET'S TAKE A HIKE!

ANTARCTICA
On no! What a terrible start to your trip! Your cruise ship has left without you! Dash across the ice to the red dinghy, then navigate the freezing ocean to catch up with the ship.
How many fellow explorers can you see?
Can you spot the bird that belongs in a hotter climate?

SOUTH AMERICA

You've arrived in Lima, Peru, and you've been invited to the Rio Carnival! To get to Brazil, trek across the Andes and through the Amazon rainforest. Then get dancing on a float!

How many llamas can you spot?

Can you find the famous concert hall that doesn't belong here?

NORTH AMERICA
Jump into this cool, classic, convertible car for the ultimate road trip across the USA. Cruise from the Hollywood Hills in California to the Statue of Liberty in New York City, where your ride ends.
How many American footballs can you count?
Which famous monument would be more at home in Paris?

WESTERN EUROPE
Don't spend too long at Madrid's famous bullfighting ring in Spain—you've got a gondola to catch! Head straight for Northern Italy and the beautiful waterways of Venice.
Every region in Western Europe takes pride in its sausages. How many can you count?
Spot the large sportsman on holiday from Japan.

EASTERN EUROPE

From Dracula's spooky Transylvanian castle in Romania, head to Russia's capital and take your seat for a dazzling performance by the famous Great Moscow State Circus. Quick! The show's starting!

How many Russian babushka dolls can you find?

Which huge ape has walked a long way from his African home?

THE MIDDLE EAST

Gallop across deserts and oilfields on your Arabian horse. Start at the bazaar in Kerman, Iran, and head to Petra, the ancient city carved out of the rocks in Jordan!

This region's famous for its carpets. How many can you see?

Spot the musician who'd be more at home in Scotland.

NORTHERN AFRICA

Starting in the bustling marketplace in Marrakech, Morocco, guide your camel across the sizzling Sahara desert to the Great Sphinx at Giza in Eygpt. A hot-air balloon trip awaits you!

How many camels can you spot?

Can you spot the icy house that doesn't belong in the desert?

SOUTHERN AFRICA
Land the balloon and climb aboard the jeep for a wild safari! Navigate the Namibian desert to South Africa's Cape Town. A seaplane's waiting to fly you around the harbour!
How many lions can you count?
Can you spot the animal which doesn't belong? It must have taken one almighty hop!

SOUTH ASIA

Hop on a mighty elephant at Mumbai, India, and ride over the world's highest mountains, the Himalayas. Finish your journey at the magnificent Potala Palace in Tibet's capital, Lhasa.

Peacocks originated in this area. How many can you count?

Find the crooked monument which really belongs in Italy.

EAST ASIA

Race your rickshaw through China to South Korea. Then paddle the yellow kayak through the busy seas to Japan's Honshū island, home of the famous Mount Fuji volcano!

How many hand-held ornamental fans can you spot?

China is famous for panda bears but can you find the bear from the Arctic?

SOUTH-EAST ASIA

Cycle from the magnificent temple at Rangoon in Myanmar through the lush tropical landscape to reach the yacht in Singapore's harbour. It's ready to go, so get pedalling!

How many traditional kites can you count?

Which monument really belongs in London?

AUSTRALIA

Celebrate the end of your amazing journey with a concert at the famous Opera House in Sydney, Australia. It's going to start soon, so why are you still in Perth? Move it!

How many koalas can you see?

Australia has some amazing animals, but which giant creature belongs elsewhere?

Antarctica: The coldest temperature on Earth was recorded here at a chilling -89.4 C (-129 F)! In fact, it's so cold that each winter the sea around Antarctica freezes, increasing its size by 20 million square kilometres—that's an area twice as big as Australia!

South America: Imagine spaghetti without tomato sauce. Imagine having no potatoes to bake and no peanuts to make peanut butter. Imagine no chocolate or pineapples! Well, thank goodness for South America. All these foods originate here!

North America: The forests of northern California are home to the world's tallest trees. The biggest is a giant redwood, called 'Hyperion', which rises an astonishing 115.5 metres (379.1 feet) into the sky. That's taller than the Big Ben clock tower!

Western Europe: The smallest country in the world is located in Western Europe. The Vatican in Rome, Italy, is tiny—only about 920 people live there! It is also the only country in the world where Latin is the official language.

Eastern Europe: The Trans-Siberian Railway in Russia runs from Moscow to Vladivostok, and is the world's longest railway. It spans 9,288 kilometres (5,772 miles) and took 25 years to build! It takes a whole week to travel the entire length.

Middle East: The ground beneath the Middle East contains some of the world's largest oil reserves. Saudi Arabia is the biggest oil-producer in the region. It pumps out enough oil every day to fill up well over a thousand Olympic-sized swimming pools!

Northern Africa: It's hard to imagine, but around 9,000 years ago, the Sahara was a place with lots of rain, rivers and green valleys! People grazed animals there, and in some places they shared the land with hippos, elephants and even crocodiles!

Southern Africa: The largest ever uncut diamond was discovered in South Africa in 1905. It weighed a whopping 621 grams! Named the 'Cullinan diamond', it was cut and polished into smaller diamonds, which form part of the British Crown Jewels.

South Asia: India, in South Asia, is sometimes called the 'land of spices'. Spices provide the tasty flavours in Indian cooking, and they also have many medicinal uses. Fenugreek can cure dandruff, turmeric is a powerful antiseptic, and cloves are used to treat toothache!

East Asia: Rice was first cultivated in China over 5000 years ago. It is an important and versatile crop used to make many things. These include: flour, bread, cakes, sweets, rope, fuel, oil, clothes, paper, beer, wine, milk, vinegar and even glue!

South East Asia: Siamese cats are originally from Thailand and were once so highly regarded that only the royalty could own them. They were guardians of the temples and had their own servants who treated them to a life of great luxury!

Australia: Many of the world's most venomous snakes, spiders and jellyfish come from Australia. The Inland Taipan or 'fierce snake' has enough venom in a single bite to kill 100 adult humans! And even the cute-looking platypus has a painful venom.

Solutions

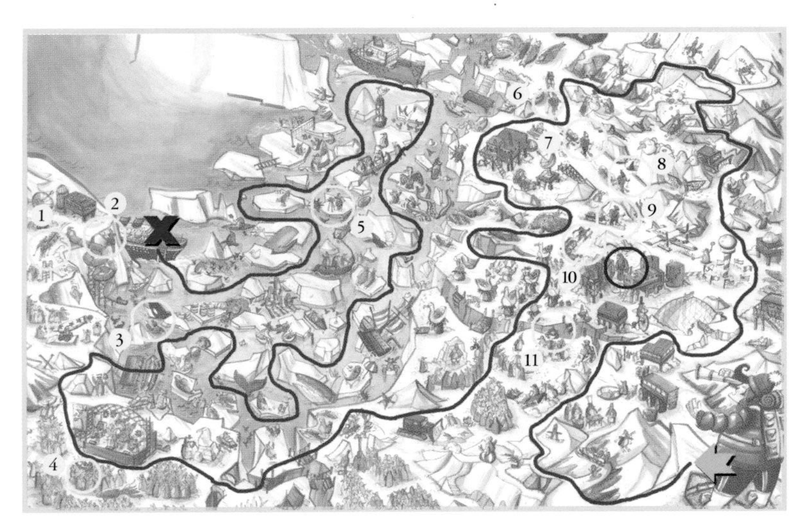

Antarctica

Find and count: 11 explorers

Doesn't belong: A parrot

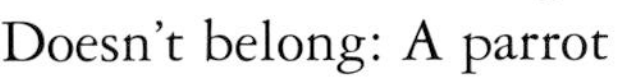

South America

Find and count: 13 llamas

Doesn't belong: The Sydney Opera House

North America

Find and count: 14 American footballs

Western Europe

Find and count: 14 sausages

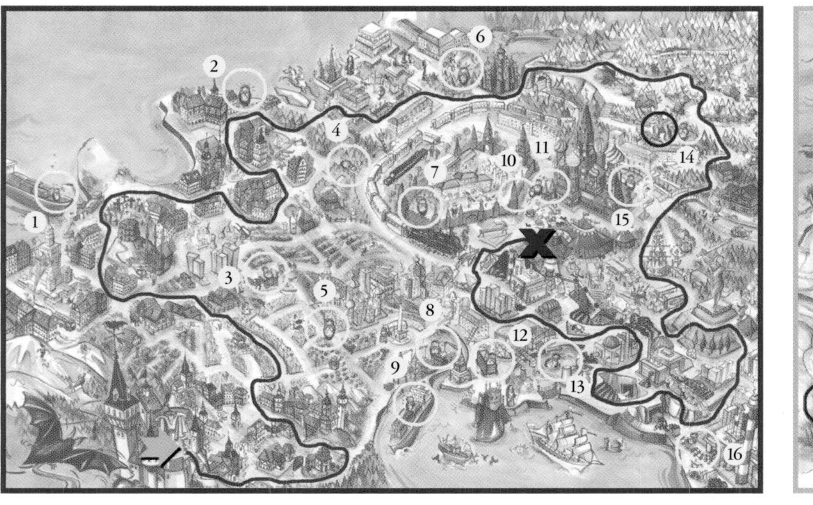

Eastern Europe

Find and count: 16 babushka dolls

Doesn't belong: A gorilla

The Middle East

Find and count: 12 carpets

Doesn't belong: The bagpipes player

Northern Africa

Find and count: 15 camels

Doesn't belong: An igloo

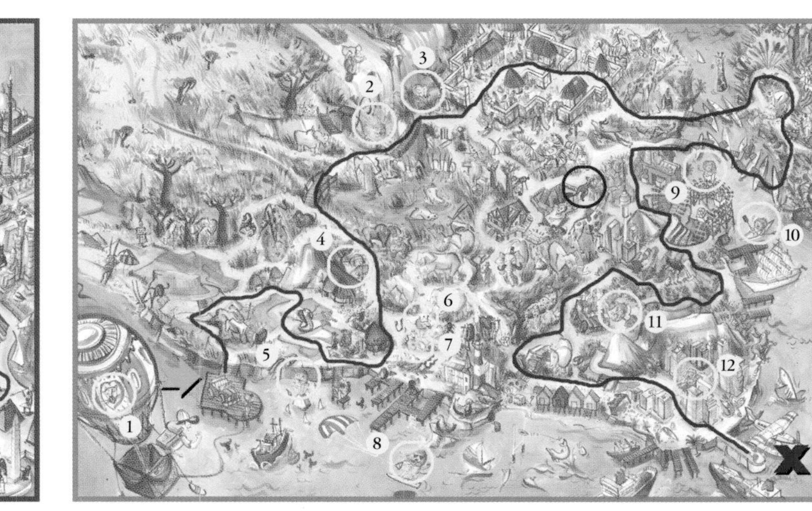

Southern Africa

Find and count: 12 lions

Doesn't belong: A kangaroo

South Asia

Find and count: 10 peacocks

Doesn't belong: The Leaning Tower of Pisa

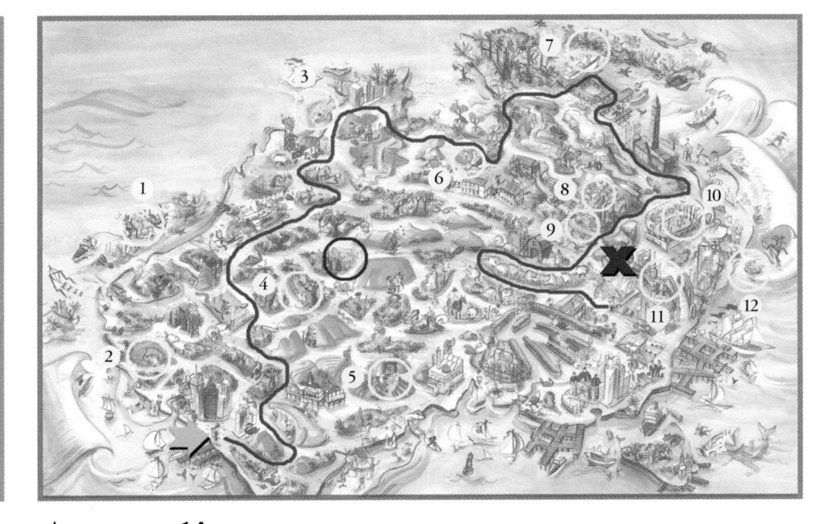

East Asia

Find and count: 11 fans

Doesn't belong: A polar bear

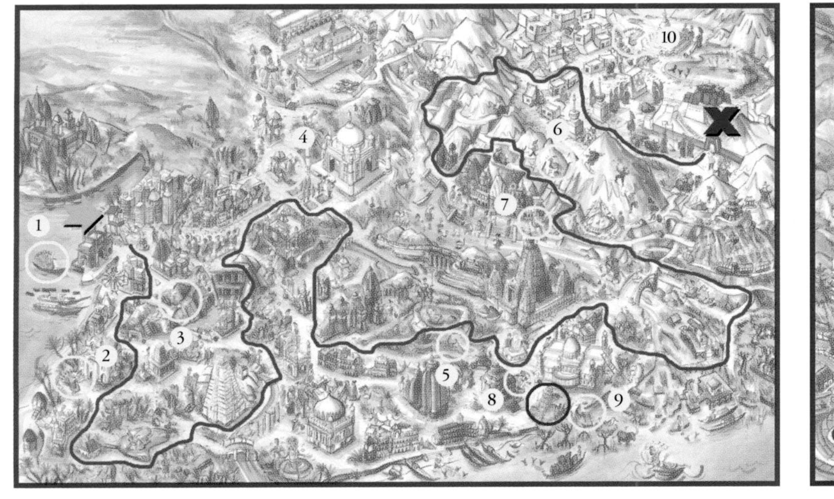

South-East Asia

Find and count: 14 kites

Doesn't belong: The Big Ben Clock Tower

Australia

Find and count: 12 koalas

Doesn't belong: An elephant